mechanical cluster

mechanical cluster

PATTY SEYBURN

winner of the 2002
The Ohio State University Press
The Journal Award in Poetry

THE OHIO STATE UNIVERSITY PRESS • Columbus

Library of Congress Cataloguing-in-Publication Data
Seyburn, Patty, 1962–
    Mechanical Cluster / Patty Seyburn.
        p. cm.
    ISBN 0-8142-0916-5 (cl : alk. paper)–ISBN 0-8142-5102-1 (pb : alk. paper)
    I. Title.
    PS3569.E88637 M43 2002
    813'.54–dc21

                                    2002007611

Cover design by Dan O'Dair
Text design by Jennifer Shoffey Carr
Type set in Adobe Rotis Serif
Printed by Thomson-Shore

9 8 7 6 5 4 3 2 1

for eric

In your vehicle, the warning lights and gauges
are grouped together on the instrument panel.
We call this grouping a cluster.

Your vehicle has a mechanical cluster.

—Ford Motor Company

contents

acknowledgments

"This Keeps Happening." *Born Magazine* (Spring 2002).
http//www.bornmagazine.org.

"The From" is forthcoming in *The Muse.*

"For" and "Choir Rehearsal, 7 p.m." are forthcoming in *Center.*

"Change of clothes? The very clothes of change!" *Western Humanities Review* 56, no. 1 (Spring 2002).

"Cambria, CA." *Trepan* 3 (Spring/Summer 2001).

"Red Level." *Crab Orchard Review* 7, no. 1 (Fall/Winter 2001).

"The Only Way." *Slate,* November 6, 2001.

"The Lady Vanishes," "(Return of) The Lady Vanishes." *Field,* no. 65, Fall 2001.

"And all the women went out after her with timbrels and with dances," "Where there is rejoicing, there should be trembling," "Both to men and to women, to every one a cake of bread, and a cake made in a pan, and a sweet cake," "Divided," "Adam Reads the Guide to Western Birds," "California Demotic." *The Paris Review* 159 (Fall 2001).

"Manifesto of Regret and Acceptance." Poetrybay.com, Winter 2000–2001.

"Wasting My Youth." *Shirim* (Winter 2000).

"Baja Triumphal." *Trepan* 2 (Spring/Summer 2000).

"Learyic." *The Seneca Review* 30, no.2 (Fall 2000).

"A Golem's Lackey." *Western Humanities Review* (Spring 2000).

"Assignment." *The Paris Review* (Spring 2000), under the title, "An Empty Surfboard on a Flat Sea".

"Death by Reminiscence," "To the Orange Still Green." *Faultline* (Spring 2000).

"Apolunar." *New Letters* 65, no. 2 (1999).

"Gem and Senseless," "Driving Tricks," "On the Waterfront" "Bell, Book and Candle" and "Exodus." *Crazyhorse,* no. 57.

"Detroit Regression," "Brooch." *Gulf Coast* 11, no. 2 (Spring 1999).

"River Rock," "Sense of Things." *Third Coast* (Fall 1998).

"Semiotics of Wind," "Mnemonics." *Quarterly West,* no. 47 (Autumn/Winter 1998).

"Facts of Flying." *Phoebe* 8, no. 1 & 2 (Spring and Fall 1996).

"Myopia in Canada." *Poetry East* (Winter 1995).

gem and senseless

The puddles in front of Speedy Muffler King request
　　　your presence, as do I. Your province, they glisten
for you (as do I), archipelago of oil and water lowly
　　　as a lentil, the manna of mourners—those wise in
matters of parable say, "the lentil has no mouth,"
　　　so survivors should not open theirs to protest death. This
empty parking lot preens, as would any pacific
　　　frill, mesa, alp or fiord, any lofty emblem called on
to connote you, stand in as your stunt double while
　　　homage is paid—we can do that, too, here at
Orchard Lake and 13 Mile Roads, orchard long plowed
　　　under and macadamized for the chassis of progress.
The lone mechanic who fixes mine asks if we, '93
　　　Ford V-6 and I, have somewhere to go, and I say yes,
but know that right now, I'll content myself with
　　　reaping the mundane in your praise—what is love,
at its best, if not ordinary? When time consents,
　　　when I've repaired all I can in one visit's camber,
I'll defy the sublime and come home, in protest
　　　of all things mournful that I've gathered in too much
ascent and descent. I will consume the legume with
　　　no ears, ignoring plangent jeremiads of the road,
and will shine like sapphires in your presence, oh
　　　my accustomed, my of course and again, my stew.

divided

It is hard to explain the light here,
earnest and aerobic light,
not the complacent kind.
It gets fired up by the ocean, and believes
in its own ability to reinvent
the vapid into the vatic,
the sore, serene,
torpor to fever,
temblor and squall to static.

I know you have light in other places.
I have lived in other places
and found curb to polestar endearing.
What can I say? Everywhere
dawn wears its mantle of emblem,
cuing insomniac, paperboy, baker.
Here in these fringe towns
yolked by Coast Highway and
the old mission route, El Camino Real,

we awaken neither more beautiful
nor more true, but the light
brings the possible on particle,
seducing the muscles and liquids of your eye.
The possible weighs little, tastes
like coriander or thyme,
and resembles its sister, the probable,
whose features are more sharply defined,
whose finest hour is dusk.

california demotic

The first word I loved was "crepusculo."
How long it took, one "u" mimicking the other,
volleyed in the syllables' canyon.
As a translation, twilight sufficed: twin "i"s
looking out, looking in, seeping rose
until night called in its chits.

My second love, "pardes," the origin of paradise,
borrowed from an ancient, civilized tongue.
It will not be given back—
the word has traveled.
Gan Eden, says Maimonides, is not
a place, but a state.

"Cordillera" tempted me,
train of mountain ranges named for saints
who battled landscape in tilda and trill.
"Horizon" (so close to "orison"—why not
bend my head?) wore a satin sash
traversing the zodiac stage.

Caged in our argot, ensnared by meaning,
we hardly hear the song of appellation:
mnemonic repetend
so like the code of peak and wave.
We keep ourselves from falling
in love again and again.

river rock

Never should I forget that in the middle of the road
there was a stone.
   —*Carlos Drummond de Andrade*

Feldspar. Mica. The language of mineral is hard,
full of consonantal conflict.
When I pace the shore, they perform introductions,
knowing I am likely to bend for identity.
But I have no more littoral pity.

Bauxite. Gypsum. No more baroque
conch fossil ore starfish to anchor my memory—
if it wants to leave, it should.
My new policy reads: be willing to let things go.
Already, I've noticed test runs at defection.

When I claimed this token from the berm,
it was between commitments,
wearing that alloyed look that a person bisected
into matter's nattering and spirit's pivot
can't resist.

Obsidian, spar. One layer recedes
from the other's edge to form a crescent moon,
attached by a vein of calcified ash.
The moon. Again. Why does it insist
on local representation? Why is everyone a movie star?

Pumice, pitchblende. Old correspondences
have flown: my stone's color woolen, texture flecked.
An alto, it sings Antonio Carlos Jobim and
smells of a wooden elsewhere—
there, I've been.

We are both unshelved. I blame luck's shell-games
(I'm always the shill but forget)
that keep me wading the bight for charms,
one ear to the shallows' minuet, the other to cessation,

and when I pretend not to listen,
the nameless drown out the named, ignite
the sky with past-tense.
This rock—I swear, my last—has the properties I love:
intransigence. Its own source of light.

adam reads the guide to western birds

" . . . let fowl fly above the earth in the open firmament of heaven."
—*Genesis 1:20*

This book is bliss.
It includes a bird's topography—
(who knew that fowl had eyebrows? *superciliaries*)
a wrist, a rump, a nape.
Once again I'm caught assuming
human privilege, as if only *our* parts merit names.
We are mere givers of names.
Parts, another parable.

It tells me the right questions to ask,
which No One ever told me.
Size? Shape? Wing? Bill? Tail?
How does it behave? Tree-climber? Swims? Wades?
Pay its bills? Struts? Darts? Variations
on the V-formation? Mating trill?
Rump patches, wing bars, patterns.
Status is rareness, and matters.

The drawings vivid, yet I could not
tell between terns
(Arctic, Forster's, Common, Least, Aleutian)—
a clue to my undiscerning nature.
Larger pictures assigned the single-sexed—
more room for androgyny in this small tome
that fits in my hand, small as if to indicate
how little I grasp, even having schooled

in that Glade. This must be
the New Tree of Knowledge, ripe with detail:
raven's Roman-nose bill, whip-poor-will's hyphens.
Ringed turtle-dove lives in L.A. city parks.

Family Mimidae are top-notch crooners.
The rose-throated becard promises
a thin, slurred whistle, *seeoo*—
I'm told that's how I sound when asleep.

I dream of Paradise: a Lazuli Bunting, a wisp
of Black-throated Green Warbler's lisp:
zoo zee zoo zee zoo (zoo lower, zee on the same pitch).
Now, with few conifers near, I will make do,
as I do   as we do
with the crow, sparrow, starling
and mockingbird that grace
my yard, their gifts of already fallen, still
falling eucalyptus and bamboo.

semiotics of wind

Make me thy lyre . . .
    —Shelley

I am concerned we are reading winds wrong
if not *all* winds, these winds
that jackknife the jacaranda limbs,
send the poisonous berries winging
like die across parsimonious felt,
rattle the power lines
and drive sparrow, dove and thrush beneath soused eaves,
scattering seed-capital and a parliament of leaves.

Suppose these whims well-intentioned,
when the zephyr puppets the branches
into flailing invitations, not knowing
that a branch lacks the arm's gift for torsion.
When it watches us perch on the couch
while our gestures divide the air from the air,
and our voices run unwitting scales in the borders,
the west wind calls, *let me in.*

There are others that threaten all kinds of displacement,
pummel the spineless, provide the local revenants with speech
to articulate dead concerns.
They give the phenomenon a bad name,
a reputation for the gothic,
when it's only a few currents, really,
some maelstrom on holiday, restless and ready to rumble.
These internecine squabbles all-consuming,

I am tempted to give up this crazy midrash.
Conciliatory, missive breeze makes an offer:
I know that walking is hard—propulsion, direction, and even the why.
Come out, and I will help you.

Stand and I will move you.
Move and I will carry you,
Sylph, on flue and flume, gust and waft.
And though we are wed by staccato and susurrus,

O uncontrollable, I can't go.

the only way

I got here by red car

via Ogallala, Echo, and Blythe, a sibyl of roadsigns
counseling against stray men in striped suits near
facilities hemmed in barbed wire

by reading solace in contiguous lines,
remedy in border

by wading states cropped in corn
breast-high, mouth-high, eye-high
though the plains flatly refused to reach up

by listening to radio preachers' static on redemption
while motel King James, spine frayed, flyleaf shorn,
advised *Turn Back, Forswear, Turn Back*

(but tell me—how could I do that?)

by manifest ambition, regret
cudgeled from decision

by Routes 8 and 10 highlighted yellow
(this the fastest, safest) yoking Mid- to West,
a jagged slash resolved to scar—is leaving

ever seamless? I got here by red car.

assignment

i.
Today's lecture on absence:
take the ocean and its glass eye.
The way waves travel, it's a miracle
they ever arrive—always late,
berating each other until
the front-runner dissipates.

Take the human and its water eye,
marrying the sea's interruptions
into a level surface that dares the peripheral:
find something else besides me.
The visionary fan flares, inclusive.
There is nothing else besides you.

ii.
I will call that wave: mine.
The pleasures of ownership cannot be measured,
though one can paddle out, skim
each saline swell, size up the height
from peak to trough, how long
for the swash to double over,
waiting at the break line—

and as you ride in, finding
the shoulder, the face, the wave
unfolds, forgiving,
even though someone once told you
he didn't know what forgiveness meant.

iii.
Today's lecture on presence:
there is no such thing as a flat sea.
Meet loss's spouse, belonging.

surf

The ocean inhales hot air from the desert
after the sun goes down. Early morning, hot and cool air collide
to fog. Intimate. Indifferent.

Before the marine layer lifts, surfers paddle out
to await the arrival of their language,
sets and crests, faces and breaks, swells, blue arcs to tame

though each lull says, *this is just a reprieve,*

no room for perfidy.
And the lithe boys are powerless among these words
that would drag them into a curl with no remorse—we'd feel better

if nature would feel at all.

A tintinnabulation of pebbles
assumes the agnostic's position: *courageous, reckless, whether or not*
you're here does not affect us

and still, the boys return in quiet camaraderie,
hoping for a glimpse of speech by low-tide,
when again they're stripped of senses, oblivious to the ocean's argot

—labial, dentate, glottal—

shapes to fill as salt water assaults lip and limb.
And when the sea bores of proselytes, it leaves
memory of tone and rhythm, the only way we know

when to end one word, begin another.

to the orange still green

Your desire for metamorphosis heard and filed away:
frustration noted, conveyed to proper authorities,
soil and rain. Issues of identity never so labored as today.
I have heard, however, if you hail from Valencia,

it's quite normal, and as far as dye—why would you
tamper with natural beauty in search of convention,
in this state where the prophetic sun anoints every
being? Merely for the sake of reinvention?

O Orange, unmatchable trochee except by slant,
by dint of the imagined word, yet to be created,
word of a new world, green world, seamless sphere
content, unbruised by fear of being belated,

join the trend—shed your insecurity, take pride
in the mother country, Brazil, in the year yours arrived
here, 1873, planted by the future scions of Riverside.
Rumor has one of three founding trees still alive,

and that could be your branch, your seed—while my kin
found themselves in Jersey City, trying their damndest
                              to speak American.

baja triumphal

i.

The sea contracts, revealing anemone that flinch on touch,
ubiquity of kelp,
starfish pointing to all five corners of the world,
away from the undifferentiated heart,
as though to say *anywhere but here.*

A floor crowded with creatures of stasis, no fish
so shallow: social algae,
a maze of mussel-covered boulders that cackle underfoot,
and sand-paths containing sufficient water to smother
what lands there.

I land there.
Rend my foot from its mud boot.

ii.

An arch thrown together quick and dirty in the last few centuries—
sandstone, red clay, debris
and a fistful of diamonds thrown overboard—
holds its own, awaiting the day
of reigning tides and tows:

under, rip, neap, high, red and low,
a day of talk between tectonic plates when the whole megillah shifts,
or a storm so ferocious that waves,
counted in stories,
beg an ending.

The ocean hides then volunteers the arch, a magician
whisking his opaque scarf from the birdcage,
bringing back the dove
he so rashly disappeared.
Guarding the ocean, the arch as yeoman—a symmetry

iii.
of tension and compression.
Am I mistaken,
or does it wear the markings of a threshold?
One we can step through and be
transformed from those without merit to those

without flaw—the great ameliators.
Nightly, when my eye sketches sleep's outline, I see
the stoic silhouette,
some minor god calcified by Poseidon's ire,
impressed into his serifed architecture.

I recognize the shape as solitude, admire it,
and remember its conditions.

cymbidium

Multiply times forty the lone bloom
recumbent in its bed of anonymous green
and baby's breath, pinned above the breast
by trembly hands—the closest they would get—
while the flash snaps this awkward vignette
into permanence.

Steal that bloom, one flare of a cymbidium orchid,
and reiterate the image, attached to a thick stalk,
on the privacy of your inner eyelid. The stalk
serves as scaffolding—it need not be particular—
its function sufficient without the flattery
of adjectives.

In high school botany, we were taught to stare
in order to see. "Sit there," said my teacher,
"and note each specific," until we'd observed,
absorbed the edges of our fears, until we became
the object of scrutiny, until the bell intoned
the end of myopia.

Now, concentration won't suffice. Tables
turned, and the orchids won't release my gaze
trained in the pedagogy of corsage—one flare,
not abundance. Pouring from a vase glazed
roseate like the bloom's promontory spurred lip,
they overflow

the eyes' containers. Is it true we're not given
more suffering than we can bear? Our neighbor
provided these questions from her garden,
pots that thrive on cement beds. En route
to the laundry room I bent to them
in praise

of progeny, lest they think a petal dispensable.
She saw me admire them, "my daughter's favorite,"
lamenting the perfidy of profligate rains,
how they feign generosity all the while
defacing the frail, and for me, arranged
blooms and fronds

in a vase we would place to upstage
an extravagance of bowls and platters given us
to fill. The daughter—did we know this?—
died last fall and now knowing this, how
the orchid changes in repose
for three weeks, longer

than its order of beauty usually abides,
exposing the survivor's guilty grace.

in a round room

In this world, beauty counts.
We know that, learn that early.
Mistrust the exceptional, until they bestow
a small graciousness.
Admire with ferocity. Assign them
more than they own—purity, kindness—since we are Greek
at heart.

As for art, we have learned how representing fools us,
have invited abstraction to our favorite restaurant
(booths, roan banquettes, buffet)
and been stuck with the check.
We are where we deserve—in a confit of confusion,
late to the century without
a polite Chardonnay.

Light slaps, slants, slips in through a broken blind,
testifies to unstinting angles.
So many can be told when words are not taking cigarette breaks.
The ocean laps, overlaps, relapses, collapses on the berm,
none of its performances the same.
Still, some will find those repetitions dull or ugly,
blame that syllable.

Gulled by doubts—"beauty" now?
When everything is gibbous?
We circle imagination,
measure its distance from delight,
argue with symmetry, embrace it.
Once again orphaned by consensus, left in Babel's hands—
striving, confounded in the hinterlands of paradise.

I love those hands and hate them,
as I do my own.

ten dodge vipers on pacific coast highway

A caravan of chassis wends the coast
along the road that bends the ocean's curves
to purpose—is it road or car that carves
intent? Avers the driver blessed or cursed?
The sea ignores the sportscars' sharp incisions.
The land, surveyed and staked or wild, cares less.
What concern of theirs, human decisions?
The metal inattention is no loss.

I know the course, have driven it too fast,
and standing still, now stare not at what lasts
but at what leaves—the freedom I knew first.
Those sound in taste prefer the ocean's rasp,
my instincts for the beautiful reversed—
(the glamorous clamor—exhalation—gasp).

four

Daily I ask four questions,
become four people.
I ask about night and the reason for difference,
about what sustains me
and what embitters.
I ask about rest, when it will come.
All in the voice of a child, who can ask
outright, who won't be told: *by now you should know.*

I stand with my arms stretched to heaven
and wisdom strikes next to me.
Though its flash blinds me
only the grass is smarter.
I exclude myself from the company of pain
and the Sea of Reeds turned red, aspiring
to no ancestry. I ask for the story
of Exodus, and understand plot, not theme.

Without language I rely on
gesture and my face,
the lintel of my brow, the porch of my chin,
to house what little I know.
Robins build a nest in my roof—I hear
their conferences on the neighborhood's merits,
if weather is clement and structure sound,
and on the warm wires starlings repeat

the same, each in their language, confused at Babel.
Where will we all find home,
a cornerstone of God's presence?
The earth's plates moan.

The sky's tablecloth drapes.
The Pacific gives explicit instructions
leaving the question of rest, a nocturne
with vigilant coda.

detroit regression

After Carlos Drummond de Andrade

For many years I lived in Detroit.
You could say, I come from Detroit.
That's why I've learned to steel myself; am realistic.
Ninety percent steel in the freeways.
Ten percent steel in the soul.
And both the desire and inability to solder my illusions.

This yearning for work that frustrates my love
also comes from Detroit: from legend and labor divided, plant and line,
        five dollars a day and lay-offs. From lead-penciled,
        white-shirted men arced over slanted drafting tables
        to draw generations of car doors and windows,
        the most important parts.
Also, this bent for invention, reinvention that fuses, infuses me
        is a true Detroit inheritance.

Have a look at my *chatchkes* from Detroit:
The steering column from a Wednesday car, a Shelby Mustang.
A forgery of Berry Gordy's autograph.
The pivotal bolt from the Ambassador Bridge.
The "D" from burnt-down Darby's marquis.
Not to mention this feigned nonchalance, this stolen shrug . . .

I used to have a red-brick house, a father, twin magnolias.
Today, postcards from Gilroy and Julian,
the garlic and apple pie capitals of California.
An avocado. A tremor. A coastal plain.
And of course, my own fallibility . . .
Not even a picture of Detroit, hard and malleable, on my stucco wall.
But how it remains!

the draftsman's daughter

Taste then was color and shape, in the reign
of convenience—orange drink and tunafish sandwiches
cut in right triangles to show the hypotenuse in all
matters, shortest path between two crusts, diagonal
connecting two intersecting roads that promise to
never meet again. On annual fieldtrips to Metropolitan
Beach, teachers plotted their own liberation, kids
practiced busride hierarchies, all city-dwellers testing
the waters of Lake St. Clair—bluer than/murkier than
others.

A savvy few knew how much clothing to shed,
baby oil to slather and submitted to the sacrament of
sun, baptism of fresh water. The rest, afflicted by
horizon, dreamed of neighborhood freedoms, preferred
the other annual outing: to Henry Ford Museum and
Greenfield Village with its antique cars, replica of
the quaint town ours never was (discontent even as
a fort), complete with penny candy and scripted
explanations of Ford's genius, the great debt we owe.

There lie our real origins: assembly line, factory,
scale and progress, $5 a day for all willing to work,
building a whole new species, trinity of man, machine
and road, a faith in destination, creed of the self-
conveyed: we were not brought here, we brought
ourselves. We feared waves' surges and tows more
than street threats, torches fueled by frustration's
kerosene, sidewalks a glass mosaic the summer
after my brother and his cinctured date went to
prom.

Belly on the floor, dolls en route to a wedding
or go-go, I watched my brother leave, I watched

the neighborhood turn on itself. Each Garden a
betrayal: conspiracy of snake, tree, fruit and God
to prove paradise fiction. If such a place existed,
it wasn't Detroit or Metropolitan Beach, and its
tenants could not be trusted–nature, we thought,
was human, for better and worse. By fiat of the
familiar, we traveled back on the bright orange bus,
limned in sand, and wanted what was ours:
the city, its riffs and misprisions.

Still, suspicion planed: seeds of something
other if not better flung far, hybrids whose roots
took hold and from my bed, I listened to siren,
alarm and bullhorn, the all-night traffic of 7 Mile
Road, imagining the lake's lyric, lake's refrain,
assembly line of face, peak, curve and froth
composing measures of departure, and I was
the bridge fording verse and chorus. While my
father drafted car doors and windows, I practiced
scale, chord and arpeggio, training my porous
ear to draft a prelude and fugue of the coast.

mnemonics

The gardeners mow, hedge and blow
        so loud and hungry that they startle the grass
        —the anesthesia of shock—
                before the blade finds its mark.
   Not that grass can feel.
Without sentience, is there pain?
   I heard the body can't remember pain.

The noise, my fulcrum.
        My brothers mowed the lawn of the 1960s,
        cleaned the sidewalk's cusp
                until the liminal was clear.
   Inside, a blur. My father in the hospital, a missing year,
the house quiet absent one quiet man.
   If there's a truth here, it's that I don't remember.

My brothers straddled our house
        to paint the chimney and stripes of maroon and white
        above the door's lintel,
                and I knew they would die
   but said nothing, censoring my fear.
They didn't worry or fall, though death was everywhere and nowhere,
        danger a rake left spoke-side up.

Men blow the fringe from the sidewalk,
        machine mouthing *more, more*
   and my heart's beat crescendoes,
                competing to hear itself as I reel
   closed the windows to quiet this reaping.
The child next door cries his voice hoarse. Will he remember
   this noise? He does not stop when the engine sleeps.

red level

i.   *I found it leaning in the basement.*
                Device for establishing a horizontal
                line or plane. Like the wheelbarrow
                in color, a working man's prop.

ii.   *His draftsman's tools gone, no straight edge or compass remains*
                Two by four, two windows bound
                slightly bowed tubes, water within,
                air bubble in each (the chicken in
                every pot) that fall between thin,
                black lines to mark the center,
                if the surface is as named.

iii.   *and the photograph of a young man in RCAF uniform*
                Two small canoes scooped out on each
                wide flat. One hole from which to hang it
                in the shop. Red paint shot with gray.
                You can lay it on its side or stand it up.

iv.   *with his cargo plane went to the future*
                Apt palindrome, each side
                meeting in the "v"—two arms
                that join at the crotch as of a tree

v.   *patriarch who loves it as he can.*
                cleaved by lightning where
                trunk and branch unite or part,
                depending on the heart's conjugations.

vi.   *My brothers find me sentimental and don't mind*
                In a gloss of stratum, red's the sunken
                shelf that shrines the gem's bathing
                gangue, vein of the unrefined pulse.

vii. say take whatever junk you want.

> Even Eliot might like it if correctly
> correlated: humble properties,
> lone purpose—to ensure an even
> surface in the face not of the odd
> but the imbalanced. Air and liquid
> kindred, wood and window wed,
> you and I, you and I level-headed,
> even-keeled, nonplussed.

viii. My mother, who remembers to forget

> Obligations to object hinge on history.

ix. and visits the cemetery often when she's lonely

> Objectivity lives in the level's
> wide-eyed evaluation.

x. wonders how she raised a child

> If I close my eyes, I see the world
> divided, not into matter and ether,
> darkness and light—into those who
> take object as subject and those
> who refuse to subject their objects
> to the mutinies of memory.

xi. with such capacity for sadness.

> What can be done but make do
> with the token left behind—
> unsold, unlauded, earns its scars

> > *— is that the person you are?*
> > *The one you blame you miss you*
> > *fear you yearn to be? Be near?*

myopia in canada

Welcome to Windsor. A big sign
for Wong's Chinese hangs just past customs.
All Detroiters go there. Her mom orders
orange food, her dad smokes Winston's, she gets
wonton soup, propels the wontons
around the bowl like boats
in a harbor with no outlets.

Her eye doctor's office
is just over the border, filled
with mirrors, frames, photographs
of models wearing glasses. She searches
his ladies' magazines, her favorite column,
"Can this marriage be saved?" and thinks that
the answers are so obvious.

Her eyes get worse and worse, she can only
see what's near. He fits her chin into the cup. So
close to her face, his hands and the machine
make her shy. He has a son her age.
She hears lenses clicking
while big, block letters become clear
and blurry—*better, better, worse.*
In thick, new glasses, she
looks smarter and uglier.

White letters jump off
green exit signs. The windshield wears
specks of dust. Everything she sees
has three dimensions, almost four,
colors begging for attention, she has to
close her eyes. *Rest, dear,* her mother says.

The family stops at Tim Horton's,
buys a box of Timbits for the ride.
Even the donuts look more acute. She acts
as though nothing has changed, because
nothing has, yet.

familiar

The gun to my ear, soon a small explosion and
a gold-plated post dotted one lobe. I was 18
and knew it would hurt, I knew that
"Your earlobes have no nerves," was
a friendly lie, a lie you embrace and pass down
as though sharing pain lessens its memory.
I read that the body can't remember pain,
but I remember the ache, a vise, a jaw-brace
with tightening screws. I'd waited so long
because I hated my earlobes, their length
and my hatred for pain, family legacies.

The "medic" at Newman's Jewelers liked pain
too much to be a healer, and he suited
the heat-seeking crowd, the woman who yelled,
"Jesus Christ!" when he held up
the gun. Ear-shootings always drew a crowd
and when I left the chair, my best friend acting
as buffer zone, two or three onlookers
touched me, to verify what they had seen, prove
I wasn't the shill in three-card monte.

Pierced, I called my mother and told her,
except about the pain, because she feels pain
for me. *"I bore a perfect child,"* she said.
"She goes and puts holes in her ears."
Much later, a lover would tell me that
length in earlobes was a sign of sensuality,
a mark of intelligence. Later still, a man held
a gun to my head, the muzzle lay
against my hair as I emptied out
my purse, wallet, pockets and took off
my ring and bracelet, scared and thinking,
I have felt this before.

the from

The Detroit Medical Center's Sinai Hospital . . . will close its doors
by September.
  —*The Detroit News*

It does not erase you, but suggests
some diminishment—
feeling slightly blurred around the edges?
As though suffering from a case of Impressionism.

Beds disinclined, machines with neon, measured
talents, plastic and elastic capabilities
to monitor, administer despair and hope,
props of reparation and delay—pairs neither
enemies or friends, but guests at the prolonging.

Where will they go? The ghosts who usher in
the newly minted, host admission to the terra firma
cinema of beat and breath and blood and
beat and breath and blood—

fire up the family camera, Sid,
your last-born wails her aria.
The levelings—entrances and exits—exchange calling cards
in fluorescent halls. On Sinai, Moses' hair palled
as he paced and awaited the good word.

And if the vacant rooms, soon to rubble,
sadden you, consider: should our places survive us?
May we outlive their leveling. So what

if we end up being born
in a parking lot, drycleaner, burger joint, five and dime,
or if the haunted bricks are left to stand

and taunt each other with *remember whens*—
bear in mind, there were we

unshelved, slapped and swaddled, taught to blink,
clutch and drive, blessed with detail and device,
all in the first few hours of life
at Sinai Hospital, scion of Detroit's northwest side.

driving tricks

I was happy for the first time
in a long while, when I reached
the hill's crest at El Moro Canyon
Road, singing—no, shouting,
gesturing with both hands,
"Brandy, you're a fine girl"
that song by Looking Glass,
a one-hit group who spun
and sounded like the Four Tops.
Brandy is some woman in a
port town who waits for her
honest but wandering sailor,
though he's told her that the
sea is his life, love, and lady.
I was driving with my knees,
I learned to do that in high school—
it's a good trick and it frees
up your hands. My pal
could drive with his teeth.
We went to Taco Taco Taco.
My soccer coach called it
"Botcho Nacho" because
people got sick there all
the time and a dead man
was found in the weedy field
next door. Another guy came
with and held my wrist to
show me he liked me but I
thought that was stupid, I
wanted my hands held, I
wanted a senior who gave
me his glasses to hold while
he drank from a cranky water

fountain and I cradled the wire-
rimmed frames in the cushion
of my palm, careful not to
stare too hard at the back
of his head. At driver's ed
we learned control, we learned
to tap the horn, the benefits
of going slow, we learned to
grip the steering wheel where
10 and 2 fall on the clock,
but I like to hook my index
finger under one spoke, see how
close I can get to letting go.

facts of flying

From so many thousands of feet,
the grid of lights and land
known as Detroit appears harmless

and organized, as though the French
and Indian settlers had a bird's-eye
plan, and with the spectral glow

of sunrise, coy and surreal behind
the wing, offered up care of the red-eye
from LA, the city looks almost

lovely, lacking in specifics
that would give a truer a picture
of this place where I was born

and lived and left, in self-declared
exile, sure I had done
something wrong, unsure of what.

As we descend, the details become
clear, and when we get closer
blur again, like the lines

on a face that you approach to kiss.

driving lessons

No parking lot with orange, immaterial
cones, we ventured forth on the feeder roads
of I-10, the John C. Lodge (so dubbed for a
dead big-*macher*), highway that siphons off
its denizens to every self-determined corner
of the Motor City. Emblems of identity   *Rochester, Romeo,*
borrowed from myth and literature 101,   *Royal Oak, Romulus*
Chippewa, Ojibway, pillaged from natives or merely descriptive:
Ottawa, Huron here's what some buck-skinned boy who
thwacked a wilderness path first saw in
the clearing—if he didn't name it for himself.

My family's last name borrowed from
the upper-crust, and they'd never know that
a Jew from Toronto adapted their assignation,
clean and British, someone born at sea in the
caste-driven past, or that their namesake would
don a white shirt with rolled-up sleeves, draft
and check fine lead-lines in service of that
noble democratist, Henry Ford, creating
"a car for the great multitudes." And when
he asked Marianne Moore for names did their   *Mongoose Civique,*
lyrical excess turn his head toward "Edsel,"   *Turcotingo, Utopian*
notorious flop? These were not words for   *Turtletop, Magigravue*
the multitudes, he thought. The name changes
the named and its purpose.

Know when to speak out, when to fit in.
I spun my web of unobtrusiveness, learned to
to laugh derisively at crash-test dummies'
demise in cars with fins older than we were
Eldorado, Valiant, and gentile movies that lauded the benefits of
Thunderbird, Riveria honking: "Gently tap the horn," spoke the tenor
of authority, "make others aware of your

presence." The honk our declamatory tool of
existence, still small voice of the boulevard. A
fellow hierophant punched my arm with
affection—I was one of the in-crowd, petitioning
at the altar of six cylinders, praying *give it up* to
the god of the pink slip or at least, his lackey
archangel,

Gabriel, Raphael,
Uriel, Michael

and on the first day of year 16, I navigated
down 7 Mile Road, past Darby's burnt-out lot,
east on Livernois, past Chippewa Party Store

Augustus B. and the neon portal of Baker's Keyboard Lounge
to Woodward's eight-lane testing ground that
sutured city to suburb, past all names I knew,
and the ball of my right foot felt the stirrings of
my exit from this city famous for strife, for its
mass-produced, affordable means of escape.

death by reminiscence

All over town, a repetition of live oaks
giving lessons on bifurcation—
they split and split, a leisurely genetics demonstration,
each inch seamlessly subsumed, no visible
divisions. How to divide

into identifiable parts en route, wanting
what's next to be worthy of what
came before, without dismissing that
as prelude, rehearsal?
Were this a problem of words, we could

parse it, but we'd have to kill
a branch to know it,
count the willful concentrics that mimic
each other's squirreling lines:
only then can nostalgia begin.

Each year I revise my list
of antecedents and results, stake claims
and pray to be believed, like the sign
for "Live Oak Road" off the interstate—the avowal
of a lone tree

hopeful, a joke or historic, my windshield nothing
but sky, a wildflower carpet and a daymoon
come to clock remaining light.
This landscape ingeniously unrolls until
I can't tell

whether the white line's fragments sing
part of the whole or *again and again.*

The insistently undead's enormity
begging attention, boughs arced
into arches, aisles and tunnels

that invite walks chaperoned by shade and chlorophyll,
beneath the umbrella of the tree's digressions.
If our advantage is mobility,
who teaches us how and when to leave?
The auguring taste of salt already

on our lips before we look back.

mechanical cluster

how far I have come
how fast traveled
slow to anger long to burn
what will protect me from
my mortal inattention
an amber state
of emptiness signal fibrillates
never enough
even when ferrying
passenger Caution and passenger Pleasure
in the back seat

a heartbeat ticks at my dictate
makes my course predictable
provisions for light
in isolation, provisos
against will and speed
those chimes and gauges needling
all decisions horizontal,
revved discordant sage
of —ometered trips
notch-numbered face
orderly as the sidereal belt
not that random model of shaken die
flung at chance on astral felt

when all goes well, we don't
look back, we heed the warnings,
make amends, we must be more
than pulse and impulse, yes?
short-circuits nerve-interpreted,
pain-relayed fuel-driven
progress we confess

to mere machinery by day's
disinfectant light but in
dark we wonder, what of
the spark? what of the spark?

celluloid iii

on the waterfront

Marlon Brando lectures on the subjunctive in the living room,
carried away with the possibility of what could have been had
    things been
different
though no one knows how different they would have to be.
                        Change responds
to increment and earthquake, depending.
The conditional is our favorite state, one with numerous borders
    and lakes,
an attractive bird, flower and motto. In California we have a
    state butterfly with
legions of supporters.
                     We must all set our boundaries,
so friends and family tell me
and I tell them back, not out of any debt to echo, though I
    appreciate
the rhetorical effects of repetition—
but, you see, we've only so much time, and we are greedy for each
    other's.
                     This is the New Greed,
which closely resembles the Old Greed and the Ancient Greed,
though the Prelapsarian Greed's another story.
I never liked Eva Marie Saint; she seems a whiner, and I don't
    understand the inversion in her last name. This film is full of
        those
                kinds of corruptions.

bell, book and candle

My mother looked like Hedy Lamaar
but I've never seen a movie starring Lamaar or Dorothy Lamour
                              for that matter
so let's talk about Kim Novak
who, says my mother, "isn't so great."

                         Sometimes we crave
     the other and sometimes we despise it.
Novak played a gorgeous witch.
We don't imagine witches looking like that—so cool blonde—
because

                         we've adopted
that crazy classical notion that beauty outside
is inside, too. She's what we'd call a "good witch"   someone
with powers
     used mainly to benefit the human race
or her close friends. Jack Lemmon, her warlock brother,
would lift his arms gracefully and turn on the streetlamps, which
I have tried,

                         without success.
Sometimes we don't need success.
They spent time at the bongo club   like poets of yore,
     or myths of poets of yore—when exactly was yore?
We used to have such nice associations:
surface vs. substance, free verse and tennis; now I can't assume
anything.

                              My mother's other
Hollywood wisdom: "Robert Taylor broke
Barbara Stanwyck's heart." It's good to have firm beliefs
     in the quotable
     when pain is at stake.

exodus

Who would expect to see Sal Mineo,

a Sabra? A testament
        to acting—never date an actor—though, who doesn't.

Sal dies and it's quite sad, could even be "tragic"
                though the Greeks have rules for that, and he's not
borne
of nobility (unless you trace his as the Davidic line),

though he is proud. Still, the movie concludes
                    on an uplifting note—really, a chord, if you're
familiar
with the theme-song, which requires a great deal of bass
instrumentation. I played it on piano as a child, a rare,
contemporary piece

found buried in the music bench, interred there
                    way before my time, and I learned it, not
telling
Mrs. Petrakovitz, whose idea of modern was Gershwin. Of course,
she was right. Paul Newman plays the leading man, "Ari ben Canaan"—
I think that means, "Lion of Canaan."

His lover's played by Miss Marie Saint—you know how
                    I feel about her, she never understands—

not Paul, not Marlon. It's a tribal conflict in that she has no tribe,
so has tribal envy. Again, wanting what is not yours
is at the heart of this
matter—now we call it desire but that word is getting so tired,

I wish the credits would roll.

white christmas

Vera Allen's wasp-waist
is this film's focus, though Rosemary Clooney's bosom is what lasted
the test of time,

                          which, we're taught, denotes
a classic. Did long-legged Vera ever trample her partner's peds?
In rehearsal, no doubt—
           her performance impeccable—
so Breck-girl, while Clooney's tones and curves implied a deeper
world, the one behind

                      the mirror, where Lilith lives—
but let's not get too mystical about Christmas. Of course, a Jew
(Irving Berlin) knew
              and wrote the score, as though
he could care about a snowy holy day. To be generous (behooving
the season), perhaps

                   he was a truly ecumenical man,
"catholic" as in universal, and suspected that Vera couldn't
carry off "La Marseillaise"
             a la Bernhardt's famed audition,
while Clooney's version of "My Yiddishe Mama" would be too, too
scorched—and
             bring on the waterworks.
What does crying tell us about a person? I know people who roll
the tears soon as

          a pup or octogenarian enters
the frame, and they're not "good" or "kind," they don't know the
right way or reason

             to feel at all, though I admit,

when the general sees his old outfit gathered in uniform to save
his Vermont Inn

                (one weekend at those prices),
singing like only the military can—"We'll follow the old man
wherever he may go . . . "—
                                        I'm a goddamn mess.

the lady vanishes

The subject is appearances—don't be snowed
by Hitchcock's smoke-and-mirrors plot
about a governess spying for the allies.
Imagine those kids, the stories they'd tell
to the tabloids: my nanny the undercover
operative, she hid a blade in her hosiery,
vial of truth-serum in her pocketbook, wore
a walkie-talkie bra. We all want our 15 minutes
and will resort to the vicarious, if need be.
I interviewed the chief justice, once, Phyllis
Schlafley returned my call and I dated a gaffer
whose crew carried lights to the stars.
Margaret Lockwood starred as the ingenue,
Iris, fresh as a big-faced, Gerbera daisy,
which played a supporting role in my own
wedding, which, if you ask anyone there,
was lovely, on a cliff overlooking the big-faced
Pacific, which, if you ask anyone there, made
the trip worth it, as well as witnessing our
public declaration of what no one can really promise.
Michael Redgrave acts the witty Gilbert,
a surprisingly modern man obsessed
professionally with the genuine—old folk
tunes and dances taken none too seriously.
(We were up on chairs, my husband was
dropped, he could have been trampled
underfoot during the *hora*, suffered concussion
while I whirled in tulle and satin—it looked
more expensive than it was). These are occipetal
habits, especially when the free world's at stake.

the lady vanishes (again)

Gilbert's sort of a tallish, cavalier, British,
less committed Victor Lazlo—Bergman's
squeeze (the saintly one) in "Casablanca"
and though they haven't much in common
it's vital to help people see how similar
we all are, unseemly idea. Things are not
what they seem: the governness a spy,
the doctor a Nazi, a gay couple who are
cricket fanatics, though cricket and sexual
orientation have no overt commitment.
Then again, they are—what they seem, I mean—
another great truth: if a man informs you
he's a loser, believe him, save yourself a world
of grief. Of course, this was the late '30s when
those vague European borders became increasingly
moot, like Michiganders from the lower peninsula
invading the upper, abandoning the "thumb"
(Michigan a hand) for parts more remote.
Indeed, this was a world of grief, though Iris
affects a quality we can only call "gaiety,"
tempered by her suspicions that evil is afoot.
She learns that it's better to be believed than wealthy,
though one's mother might say, you can't
eat belief. We trust the couple won't starve—
they are slender and tall, the first signs of
good-breeding, the lozenge that's supposed to
protect you against the barbarous, but they drink
too much tea and so would suffer in battle
with a wound. In extreme times, don't maintain
old habits. In black and white, blood can be
nuance. In a country called "Mandrinka"—
(backdrops clearly Switzerland, decidedly Zermatt,
telltale Matterhorn, chalets galore) one must
locate an ally even in war between the sexes.

(return of) the lady vanishes

"I've no regrets," says Iris. "I've been everywhere
and done everything . . . eaten caviar at Cannes,"
(her champagne reacts, the bubble size attests
to quality) " . . . sausage rolls at the docks . . .
baccarat at Biarritz . . . what is there left for me
but marriage?" Her friends have been reading
Byron and rebuke her for no mention of love,
reading Buber and console her with "I and Thou,"
reading Nietzsche and try to convince her
not to settle—their valises laden with language's
weight and theories of existence. She descends
into the underworld and emerges with a man
in tow, the lady Orpheus only it worked this time,
she marched straight ahead, as the modern
woman does—no regret for this Lot's wife.
The secret? A tune, a war-winning code that
dear Miss Froy (the spy) memorized—we heard it
twice: during the opening credits and again outside
her window—but we did not pay attention because
we have forgotten how and like this film's Brits,
we ignore clues, caught up in our ceremonies,
bought and paid for, deceived by our digressions,
charmed by the camera, its wily angles, while
the leitmotif taps on our shoulder, and myth
nibbles our cuffs. We are eroding, inattentive
while Miss Froy is drugged and wrapped in bandage,
awaiting a fate we can't let ourselves imagine—
death incorporated exit stage right never say never
endless night. I dreamed of being married
while crossing a fictive border, my subconcious
craving the most mundane metaphor, one
state into another. What puts the plot into
motion is an "avalanche" in ambiguous Europe

and soon you have a train, sneering Germans,
an importunate porter, infatuation banter—
oh Froy! Oh Freud! Such fantasy. In real life
the lady doesn't vanish until after the wedding.

ketubah | iv

All is valid and binding.

"both to me and to women, to every one a cake of bread, and a cake made in a pan, and a sweet cake."

Climb down, said the angel of the Lord
in banquet-waitress raiment (black skirt, white shirt)
to the plastic pair.

To make the trip, they broke apart.
They'd never been apart.
Arm and arm in symmetry—one dark, one fair.

Bound by ropes of icing at each edge,
a minefield of piped fleur-de-lys en route,
they skimmed the surface to the fondant cliff,

repelled the height of each genoise
laced with brandy (so airy, light), three tiers
of augmenting circumference stiffened

by invisible pillars, and into
night's whorls, disappeared.

The baker's wife told the irate parents:
someone stole them. To the baker, she said:
this keeps happening. Growing accustomed to defections,

he nodded, imagining the groom
awash in layered buttercream and ganache,
tokens of confection,

licking frosting from his bride's pumps,
she from his undenoted fingers,
smeared in joy. And the Angel of the Lord shed

her uniform and slept

with a small white box for a pillow,
and the slice contained fed

her dream of a ladder from earth to heaven,
of men and women
ascending and descending,

ascending and descending
and they were sustained.

"where there is rejoicing, there should be trembling."

i.
Let the glass we smash be doubt,
the wine free will,
the bouquet, a mosaic of mercies.
On ritual's stage, each prop represents.
Symbolic as the Red Sea's courtesy:
the miracle was faith—not dry land.

Make this a day of amnesia
when we forget tattered truths and lidded counsel, caution's wraith,

the Angel of Death's demands.

ii.
It has taken this long for me to forgive
story for reducing to the sauce of lesson.
That's how I knew I was ready to marry:
I stirred and stirred, and the punditry
burned off like sherry.
What remains is the echoing crackle of the glass

wrapped in linen beneath my lover's heel
as we frighten the demon, shatter the temple, the hymen, the silence,

part and parcel of the past.

"change of clothes? The very clothes of change!"

i.

The train, a flume of white satin, flares
from an empire waist—bust of bead   pearl—arms
bare as the wait is long restless, days dissipate in seamless
collusion and the tulle slip sighs as the dress fastens:
hip rib breast.So am I immanent:
possessing possessed.

ii.

Hardened to marble,
Kore Venus Juno carved and garbed to last
a millenium or three. Identities defined by prop gown hair—Rome's
empresses
known for nose style and the rare appellation,
"Maconiana Severeiana," scripted in those
popular triangles. Inscription
gives her the edge over
other girls goddesses
vitual ciphers
(stones in their eyes pilfered)
few symbols left to decipher. Only their images
remain—or less—Severiana's container adorned with Ariadne Bacchus—
revelry unrestrained except by the myth
of fixity.

iii.

How perplexed my people
were then—one God with many sects,
fused only by assemblage of holy texts, temple
soon to fall to Rome—rejecting the once future messianic elect.
Nonetheless, they'd survive sans avatar idols nymphs
numerous as stars confined
to constellation—firmamental scars

of love war metamorphosis—changing
of the spiritual guard: girl to tree willow rain spider cow nightingale
before they knew—before it was true—that you can't
change anyone unless she wants to change.
Success evades ultimatum's duress.

iv.
The mathematics of marriage
a mess—two to one to two—are we now
part or whole? I bought this dress that sways slightly
to impress my image on the eye of an August late afternoon
slated for a provident daymoon that shows its face no sooner than
Bach's third Brandenberg regales the room.
As for these vows
impugned for their naivety—did you
assume me unaware of human failings cruelties
tendered mended unpent vented repented unrepented? I intend
them to last as least as long as Getty's statues crypts busts.

And if—and if this plan goes wrong,
I want to know it when—not before—dress
returns to worm, only hem's memory grazing the floor,
my form refashioned as dust.

"on the wings of every kiss . . . drifts a melody so strange and sweet . . . "

You have heard the words at least
72 times, the median
needed in order to learn them,
but since I am
"In a Sentimental Mood"
prescribed by Milt Jackson's vibraphone
and apparitional jazzers lounging
on my couch, I will say them again and again,

true and tried, tempting banality.
We may as well chide the spiderweb's construction,
thread after thread until the parlor's done,
and beckoned, the fly gets its reckoning.
Our words catch us. Our notes reel us in.
Repetition is petition,
petition is prayer's twin
and prayer is faith's cousin,
the quiet, good-looking one

and that's why we are here,
ready for portents.
If it rains, we'll claim it cleansing.
If bright, we'll say, of course.
If cold, the better to see the breath of words.
Leave irony in the back seat, in the trunk.
When Milt plays "At Long Last Love"
the keys do not complain as he finds them
again and again, each touch
discrete, each tone in its float,
each revel crescendo unrivaled.

Missing one thread, the web's less effective—
minus one kiss—why subtract that?

Assurance the province
of creatures and gods.
No shame in excess.

". . . and all the women went out after her with timbrels and with dances."

At my wedding, my father, ten years dead,
practices what Isaac Babel called
            the "genre of silence"–that is,
            he says nothing.

And the art of invisibility, which
he has mastered.

Unseen, unheard. And I don't look or listen
for him until my sister begins to cry,
            and my mother accompanies her,
            lovely in her suit of lavender years
            and satin trim,

women who remember, remind,
who mine

today's gold-flecked soil for veins
of remorse, who forge timbrels
            from sand-dollars'
            fragile intaglio.

We ask my father to dance   in the dimming
nimbus of light.

"rise up my love, my fair one, and come away . . . "

En route to Ave Maria at 10 a.m.
                              crosses as flags, flags as crosses, the holy
perpendicular
mingling in the vault

closer to the pulpit as Pentecost nears,

the north 405's splendor makes
itself manifest—timing rules
when it comes to revelations:

the female whale helium balloon banked halfway between firmament
                                        and car dealership.

She is steadfast—repeatedly
the fine citizens of Garden Grove shoot her down and the owner
patches her up and floats her

to draw motorists' gaze to his wares, and she begins
to acquire civil rights of her own—
                              a square of air, a current—to represent

 the most plastic perseverence:
                      yielding and unyielding,
unconditional.

Our friends, one
in white, one
in black,

kneel and accept what we cannot

and the priest dusts even the nonbelievers with an affable blessing

so we are saved, for the moment,
                              from our remove.

I say, anyone who wants to pray for me
can,
so long as there's nothing to sign and my soul goes unclaimed.

Everywhere a Mary a host of votives
                    long drinks of stained glass to soothe
              the parched narrative,

Twelve Stations of shard and burden,
lacunae between
man as God as man. A billboard at turn-

of-the-Century Boulevard sacrifices
its doubts to Octavio Paz,   *The Road Never Stops Arriving*
              and as we wend

the streets of a long-ago mission town, Paz's line
lingering on my shoulder like the voice of conscience,
              that faithful toucan,

the day's messages declare themselves
                    holy, holy, holy
                              kadosh, kadosh, kadosh.
When I hear these words I rise
up on my toes as my faith,
              pacing in the anteroom, teaches,

a mere fraction of the morning's signs and symbols
—I want
      to grab them all

              for my friends as a pledge that they are not
"alone together"
hopelessly fallen, driven, lost in a jumble of gesture of vow

as a pledge that the world
is with them—which
you don't know and you never know.

V

If you abruptly release the accelerator
or brake hard while going too fast
around a severe curve, your vehicle
may change its direction of travel.
—Ford Motor Company

If we all pulled in one direction,
the world would keel over.
—Yiddish proverb

a golem's lackey

The eye by which I see God
is the same eye by which He sees me.
    —*Angelus Silesius*

My master says he wants you to leave him alone.

He says your demands are excessive—he cannot cleanse the city
streets of spit and graffiti pen invectives mend the well-water pails
hurl persuasive pamphlets bully Cossacks into submission and
eviscerate stray demons (satyr and scylla, nasnas, lamia and manticore)
all in one day. He complains of exhaustion, can't catch his breath, has
pains in his shoulder and jaw.

He says you should know better
than to employ him for trivia.

He rails: You Solomon ibn Gabirol, Maharal of Prague,
Eleazar of Worms, all of you who dangle from history's hook because
of me, your rules—don't let a boy under 30 study Kabbalah—are fool-
ish. And after 30, when a man meets his limits and takes turn hating
himself and his creator? Only a child under seven—six days the world
took—should be able to create.

He says you should know better
than to have made him at all.

He speaks to me without voice
I hear him in the interstices of consonants, the vowels' wells

I hear him in the ledding's walls
I hear him

He says if he has no soul, that's not his fault. If he has no heart, he's not to blame. While desirable, they'd find no home in his body's dank clay. He says that his favorite city in Italy is Florence due to the statues, with whom he converses and promises vainly: your day will come.

●

He says liberation was once a train's whistle
but now he won't take trains.

●

He says I must protect the letters on his forehead, *emet,* concerned that a sage will steal in while he sleeps and revise one word to another—truth to death. Before I die, I must smear the word, render him inert until another cleans its grooves. He says it is a great honor that I must keep secret. That most great honors have a shameful countenance.

●

He quotes Talmud:
"Three come unawares—
the Messiah, something found, and a scorpion."

●

He speaks without moving his mouth.
I hear him in the dust my feet raise en route to shul
I hear in him the dust
I hear him

He shows me a shade plant, zebrina pendula—"wandering Jew"—and says that Cain was once a handsome, simple man. That people should know: God means consequence. He remembers when Ezra the Scribe redacted Torah, and they used his index finger as eraser, fitting narrative to theme, reforming the story.

He says no story that keeps your attention is true.

For what purpose was I created?
Homonculus's assistant, servant to the man
manmade, translator of what can never be
articulated? His speech decants I drink
and hear the liquid of scripture forbidden
I didn't ask for this I am of a slow tongue
how rarely we ask for what we're given

He says my training with him is good practice for *olam ha-ba*
where I will listen all day to prophets who have traded woe and charge
for poetry and when I tell him I don't believe in the world-to-come he
covers my full face with his hand so that God

cannot see me

Eighth Day

Between steel strings and hammers clothed in felt,
between fret and neck, tongue and reed,
black sharps and flats of the soul,
(where else would spirit reside but in tones' anterooms?)
between uttered speech and the uncluttered
argot of the heart, its bass percussive,
exists an agreement, a contract.

Between the ardor of blood and veins' cerulean flumes
fashioned for travel, between fontanel
and its thin shawl of skin, initial display of fragility,
in the interstitial demands of bone and ligament,
between conduit neck and the head it bends acutely
in prayer, in these ceremonies of need
a contract exists, an agreement.

And the Lord offered Abram a covenant,
"between Me and thee and thy seed after thee."
And in his tents Abram mused,
and in desert terms, the Hebrew of five stones
smoothed by the river Euphrates,
Abram loosed the most human of questions,
What's in it for me?

and God poured Himself into language,
the very vessel that He confounded
at Babel, a glottal obstacle course
of verse and reprise.
He ran scales, inversions, arpeggios
and replied, improvising a riff of faith:
Nations. Land. Eternity.

The child sets out, a blessing clutched in one fist;
in the other, a token of loss, a tear that dissipates

into the elements' contract, agreement of atoms
to cohere in rage and bliss.
Nothing consists of just itself:
there is fear in righteousness; glimmer in grief.
When He breathes life into newborn

nostrils, they open to all this.

brooch

Take this round blue enamel universe
how complete   with its jeweled moon and Milky Way
affianced to the lapel of stylish Bernice at 90
at 90   the firmament aligns on her bearing
once trivial in the glitterati glass case More stars she bids
More stars   all blue as Blake's imagination wild
in purity Bernice's Ford Falcon red as faith
her hair white   as waiting her gait stealthy
as a Dakota girl's soprano devoted to prayer
emanating   from the vessel of her throat
Beckoned she climbs a dream ladder sees
Jacob's heels   seventy elders beholding
God's feet "a pavement of sapphire stone"
her azure eyes   gaze she chooses to leave behind
what pins her to this world our token days

for

Homage envisioned, centered two-thirds
        from the moat where we fall from the page's
        estate into air's container, I watch him
            sleep, the lover's privilege—obligation (visage
     unencumbered, lines surrounding eyes
        and mouth less pronounced, night's language
        kind and fricative)—a free show
            that consistently refused, indicates a lack
                    of compulsion—what is love without that?

Three clerestory panes provide adoptive
        light (that we did not invite but accept as our
        own)—my gaze adapts to scarcity,
            rewarded pupils wide. This preposition,
    workhorse, shorthand, must encompass
        honor, debt, exchange—this book
        offered up (my ram, my grain, my gold, my child
            narrow-spined, so thin but cheeky, never
                shutting up)—give me him, though it's not

an even trade, my gains exceed my lines,
        numbers, beats and stresses, rooms
        —but who would balk at this imbalance?
        He is the equation's X, and Y
    must figure ways to calculate his constancy—
        what is love without that? I did not expect
        to be a brooder, wondering how long I'll have
            this all, all this, how long to stare—perhaps I should
            shake him awake, in case the wayward

angel declares *time's up* before the daily
        radio can blare and our souls docily return
        to awkward frames. I don't concern myself
            with hell's flames or heaven's unguents,

instead fear soil's frigid grip.
      Is it wrong to use the other as a foil?
      Remind, remind me I'm alive, I say,
          and he complies—what is love without
             compliance? If happiness is trite, grotesque,

a facile challenge to misery perfected
      and contained within the heart's protective
      cavity, an affront to doctrine and intellect
        (high-style evasions)
I don't care. I'll hold him on this page
      secure in ink's obdurate embrace,
      despite, to spite the cancer of disdain,
        and worse, invasion of the vast estate
          of nothingness—believers, dis- and non-, erased.

apolunar

To orbit the moon and find
                the point farthest from her
center. We turn from each other,
                slacken to solitaire. So begins
our nightly antiphony: she calls out
                an order, we respond—only
we call, too, and she follows suit,
                invites the centripetal force key
to whatever is inevitable.
                Aside from lunar talk, I can't
explain why we cleave
                and cleave, divide and smother,
find a limb and toss it
                back, roll to the abysmal cusp
where blanket, sheet and pillow
                have abandoned tack. The motions
stir me from my petitions to Morpheus
                for bland dreams or none, to Tyche
for fate and fortune I can
                stand, withstand, understand.
We don't trust Yahweh
                to manipulate love's levers, favor
the ancient division of labor:
                Oh glowing goddess of flattering light,
adroitly cast your clever angles,
                your antimonious sheen
on the catwalk of romance. I'll cede
                to your revolutions so long as when
we turn and counterturn, we end up
                in countenance, distilled
from sleep's chaotic vat.
                "We're all the wine of something,"
tips the poet, tips the glass—
                but tell me, oh bright instigator

overseeing kiss and fumble,
oh pundit above, oh celestial
barkeep of the dark matter
in universal margins, can you
explain the fermentation of love?

After Marie Ponsot

don't come to me

as a shower of rain
like Zeus to Himalia,
nymph of Rhodes,

as a bush that burns
unconsumed and
mouthless, speaks,

as gold that preens
inside the gangue—
shows of mineral

passion, element follies
catch my eye but will
not win my mortal

affections. We need
no longer endure
the clumsy hands

of transformation,
like sister constellations
tethered to epic whim

that lauds the slow
and lovely who gave
up corpus for star.

a bedtime story

Don't hesitate to say you are not in love.
We are not Greek or Roman anymore.
No Cupid, Aphrodite or Juno will strike you down.
They may try to woo you with arrows, potions or hearsay,
their favorite chariots.
They may praise you for your unwillingness
to call what is not love, love.

Many sophisticates prefer other appellations,
such as "adore": "I adore you, you know."
They, too, are exhausted—a singular exhaustion—
that of the replica, slightly wan,
subleased by The Euphemist
to those in need.

Once elite, now common as flapjacks.
You must pity them, so misused.
That would be terrible, wouldn't it?
In perpetual service of intention falling short.
"The romancer's prosthesis."
Can one really be saved "by the love of a good woman"?
Are there princes roaming the coastal plains?

If only as collateral,
consider voting yes.

at cucina stagionale, my aunt lilith
starts to cry

for S. T.

when our waiter asks if we'd like to "start" with antipasto.
Though the bad girl of Midrash, being born in a textual gap
(Genesis 1:27, to be exact) has made her sensitive to issues
of origin. Prone to apocalyptic prophecy, buoyed by Chianti,

she sputters and spouts Ezekiel: "And they shall . . .
execute judgments upon thee in the sight of many women!"
"Calm down," I say, and mutter a quick "Out Lilith!"
which keeps her in her chair. Really, she's a family friend—

thank God, not my blood.

Old as old gets, she looks good, plucks thick strands of her
black hair—*tresses,* she hisses, slips one into an expectant
mother's glass of milk, which would kill the poor thing,
if I weren't there to fish it out. "Must you act this way?" I ask

after another perfidious day. She shrugs. "Something to do."
She claims the house's protective mezuzah defective,
that the girl wore no amulet. Lilith's got an eye for loopholes.
For that matter, keyholes. She glances at my water glass.

"Don't even think it," I say.

It's not that she's lonely, married to Demon King Asmodeus,
who, if remote, at least treats her as an equal—unlike Adam,
for whom she still pines—so hard to forget your first love,
isn't it? Though he's done his best to leave her behind, even

got her booted from scripture, except for that small slight
in Isaiah, a note in apocrypha, cautionary tales—her every move

fodder for medieval folklore—Lilith sews an evil dress,
Lilith hypnotizes virgins, Lilith spawns a thousand demon

children. "Don't remind me," she says.

And don't mention E- or the G- (Adam's former rib and
their living situation, albeit temporary). She gets livid,
looks for infants to strangle, men to seduce out from under
conjugal sheets, cutting a swath of unfettered desire

that may as well bear her blazing initial. For me, the Sabbath
is no day of rest; that's my shift, when I give the angels—
Senoy, Sansenoy, Semangeloff—a break from exhausted
guardianship. I tell them, "Take a load off your peds,"

and there's nothing like a grateful angel.

Not that it's hard to find her—she lives in the mirror,
yenne velt, the other world. When I come to summon her,
I catch her unawares, pruning her hair of contraband gray.
"Am I allowed no dignity?" she sighs, but lets me stay

so long as I promise not to touch anything, infect her
home with warm-blooded remorse. You'd be surprised
at the rooms inside a square, reflective plane—a virtual palace,
plush and redolent of sandalwood but silent as ice—

an exile's domain.

bartender cain at the alibi lounge

You're right, I tell you, and *no, it's not fair.*
You look up, feeling dubiously bolstered,
surmising that I understand, or care
as proven by my advocating shoulder.

The brutish facts assault you 'round the clock:
No righteousness, no justice, little mercy.
Abel offered up the firstlings of his flock.
I proffered my tilled fruits, and God cursed me.

I don't know how I got this rotten job.
I suppose it's because I killed my brother,
I dole out feckless comfort because God
has labeled me eternally the other.

A toast to all the fools expecting more.
A drink to those surprised by sorry lots
whose friends and family they often bore,
lamenting, *You're the only thing I've got.*

this keeps happening

Sister, quoth Flesh, what liv'st thou on, Nothing but meditation?
—Anne Bradstreet

A hunger prodded me awake before dawn,
before the paperboy smacked our porch with news.

No garden-variety, esophageal yearn,
it has radiated to my hips, eyelids, ankles, follicles
and fingertips, the nails— even calcium, it permeates.

In my shoulders, their scaffolding.
The hanger of my clavicle.
Such contagion, and I have just eaten breakfast.

Perhaps a grasping at answers: what happens after
body and soul part ways?
Where are my lost props and spells?

Could it be simple desire, this century's kiss,
or greater—sympathy for those unmoored,
or smaller—a pinch of boredom?

What about that craving for a personal god,
half-idol half-ether
to patrol the dark matter?

Such questions, moot. It is not even
lunchtime, yet and every cell in my cooperative

complains of emptiness. They think I have control,
what with the brain and all at my command,
the heart's imperatives, intention touring my joints.

How can I explain this helplessness?
No salve, manna, nectar— no wonder my hands have
aged, taking dictation from such clientele.

choir rehearsal, 7 p.m.

From beaches Huntington, Newport and Long,
    from island, peninsula, ranch and mesa,
        we venture inland
           to Westminster, to Bet David—House of David,
    clerestory views and 40 wooden pews,
    after the anointed
        who calmed Saul with harp and song.
    Please come singing, says our cantor. *Please come ready to sing.*

In the room behind
    the holy scrolls, the ner tamid, the stained-glass parables,
        robes in closets smooth their voluptuous
folds,
        and two rows of chairs unbend at the waist.
    The cantor lifts her slender arms
    to let us know it's time, reign in
        transgressions, keep our pitch in tow.
    Few miles west the ocean cues

a coda in its canon, high notes cresting white.
    "The waves are running in verses," says Miss Bishop,
        who is usually right.
        Nearby, the 405: syncopated friction
    of wheels on unseen stripes, horn riff, muffler, radio,
    siren, tire bursting seams, alarm, squeak and squeal,
        they fill our fermata
with the gush of chance music

like the stone struck by Moses's staff,
    giving forth more water than the Hebrews could imbibe.
        Too much or not enough:
        water, manna, quail. Love, money, time.
    Six days of work, one of rest;
    six of toil, one of singing—

to keep the excess dammed? At bay?
To separate, on our minor scale, light from dark,

as we are Makers of list and label,
phylum and genera, branch, strain, and fable to explain
what exists outside the world we contain:
recall the old scholar, who, while he prayed,
could not be taken by the Angel of Death.
Said angel cast a stone in his path.
The man tripped, gasped, his chant abated,
and the angel, riding the broad brim of his hat,

made his move, invaded.
Would that we could stave him off!
Sea and freeway hem us in;
unless our notes reach up, they'll be consumed
like Pharoah's soldiers in the Red Sea's folds.
Please come singing, says the cantor. *Please come ready*
to sing.
Listen: not for deliverance, not for wind,
rain, footfalls or forgiveness from sin, but for
the still small voice in each imperfect hymn.

learyic

For pain, balloons of nitrous.
For comfort, errant debutantes.
For solace, information webs
and nets to hold the words
that flee your brain's confabulations after all these lucid years
the brain you'd not consign
to cryogenics' nagging clipboard.
No waves—sine or oceanic, tsunami, effluvial, no tempest could
encompass what transpired
inside, beneath, around the lobe,
elusive, primed and porous.
Avoiding measurement the way
to say that what we test tells less than what's impossible to test,
the underbelly   of the palimpsest.

sense of things

Loose air ellipses from the open fist.
Wind chimes tuned to Chicago blues
five notes refuse

to resolve a chord due to brackish winds,
breeze's beck, the ocean sullen
with white spume.

Nature hates a vacuum, just ask and
you'll conceive. How can you even think
of raising an idea

in this neighborhood, with all these
sinister trees and cul-de-sacs? The world
is a poor fit. All the tailors

on Carnaby Street, Rue St. Faubourg
and Seventh Avenue can't do anything.
You'll have to grow into it.

curriculum vitae

I had thought, perhaps, voluptuary in training,
collecting postures and a surfeit of whims
but my goals were restricted by tariff, tort
and other guests of profit, which has always
                          resented my attentions.

Employed in the business of trap and parabola,
a local daddy-longlegs caught my eye in its web
and my thoughts spun to stained glass,
a numinous profession. I studied and won

some acclaim but lost too much blood
as I practiced my craft—my shards palled
in sympathy and any paned window pained me—
its divisions, competitions, abuses of light
                          in service of refraction's tyranny.

The black box theatre called. I considered a number
of one-woman shows—my life as a Campfire Girl,
my life as a pyromaniacal teen, my life as
a sci-fi ingenue, the skateboarding pizza girl

of cyberville. I willingly invaded my privacy and banished
the squeamish to memoir. Just my luck,
the persona union went on strike for its annual
suspension of disbelief increase
                      and Lord only knows when they'll settle.

I entertained faith-related ambitions.
To test the waters, bitter like those
the adulteress drinks or sweet as apples, nuts and wine
masquerading as mortar, I asked for

guidance. Adam Kadmon showed up in his usual
primordial state, carrying an armful of numbers,
but soon my small congregation went in search
of someone taller with a finished rec room
                              and solid criteria for prophets.

I was mixing V-shaped drinks and refilling
peanuts, cheese and cigarettes amidst
scions of modernity when Schoenberg met Gershwin
and scheduled their first game of tennis

and I spilled not a drop, not a drip.
I lifted stoles from the ivory shoulders
of Isabella Gardner and Sarah Bernhardt
and did not trip, sputter or dip
                              but was fired for subordination.

In spare time I invented the gesture, the cubit,
the bottom rung of a ladder—we each have
our own weight to bear. I bred a genus
of the new dirts, which gave me a hand in fertility
                              and now, so much looks familiar.

My start-up business sold home-made
gingham, jam and leaf-tea but local sibyls
used my wares to predict imminent plagues
and yard sales while neighboring merchants

declared my spreads taciturn, fabrics prone to bunching
at pulse-points, searching for heat in the face
of cooling passions. For a fashion magazine
I researched the history of tulle but was given
                              no tulle in return.

Once, I had direction but squandered it. As a child
apprenticed to a lutier and a cartographer,
I could not carve or draw a proper curve,
could not fret the neck, and tended to enlarge

the states I preferred. With Doublemint wrappers
I built a city inside the maw of my desk,
complete with skyline and scatter-side housing,
a mall, a fountain and streets organized in a grid.

                              All during lunch and study hall.

Through it all, bless-her-heart my mother professed,
"You can be anything you want."
Success in my family defined like obscenity
according to the Warren court:

we know it when we see it.
How I took her confidence to heart—
the American dream, mine
to live, mine to sliver! Stapled to their telephones,

my references await your pledge.
Calypso's sisters, they sing my gospel
in gorgeous voice and have won me
many a position. Please call early, call often

                        and frame your questions as multiple-choice.

manifesto of regret and acceptance

I apologize for being late.

I meant to get here yesterday in time to say
what he said.

My affection for meaning should not affect you

dreams—a precipice, a cliff

though I lament that it means something
to you who don't mean.

I apologize for guilt
and feigning guilt, the *mea culpa* I don't mean.

I apologize for Latin

a language "dead as dead can be/ it killed
the ancient Romans/and now it's killing me"

quoth my father, may he rest in peace,
wherever peace may be, it's not where he was buried
at 8 Mile Road and Woodward
(near the Michigan State Fairgrounds)
and incidentally, Latin did not kill him.

I apologize for death.

For introducing death,
who sews his number into cuffs and hems
in case we need to call.

I apologize for never having clapped.
For thinking, maybe Tinkerbell should die.

(So small.)

For asking: if less is more, then what is more?
By definition, more than less
though what will last is anybody's guess.

I have suspicions—who are you?
You are anybody, too.

(So frail.)

I won't apologize for my parents
and you shouldn't either—you didn't
make them that way—like Larkin said,
their parents did. The same goes if credit is due.

I won't apologize for being a Jew—

all we did was jettison some excess gods,
perfect the allegory, build a temple, build another

with a wailing wall
and on occasion, wail
when the wall reads its messages
and calls (all too often) for grief.

I won't apologize for awe

though it's difficult to carry and refuses to fly
even harnessed, through the air

which, near the ocean,
is fit for lungs of gods
filtered through a parliament of urchins.

I apologize for some belief
in God,

at least enough that bouts of doubt are departures.
Such convictions do not keep me

from irony parties, at which
cookies shaped like stars are served
and beverages are bittersweet.

I apologize for fear fire fanfare

for ire err desire

for flies lambs limbs

and all the others sacrificed
with no wine to wash them down.

We can't hide time's keys forever.
Eventually, space will wake up.

Know now: I meant to get here yesterday
before the proclamation, admission, petition

so I could make one myself.

wasting my youth

"And God saw that it was good."
   —*Genesis 1:4, 1:10, 1:12, 1:18, 1:21 1:25, 1:31*

" . . . Behold now, I have taken upon me to speak unto the Lord,
   who am but dust and ashes . . . ."
   —*Genesis 18:27*

i.
Already, I have spent too much time
bargaining with God, wooing dissolute angels,
slicing the heels from rye loaves
to use bread's most tender matter
for their pickled tongue sandwiches.

As though He is waiting for me
to slip up, as though I merit such attention,
my verbs and doubts recorded in the Book of Life
we cite on holy days, slights and sins
penned by a hirsute amanuensis,

I check cold burners for spare blue flame,
run wicks under the faucet's flume,
chew salubrious root, with every sense I barter
for another hour, crease of light,
in praise, ashamed of what I have

—it is so good—
which He claimed (repeatedly) during week one,
                                    those opus days.

ii.
I'm waiting, too, worried that He'll find
flaw untenable, clean the slate, noting
firmamental clause in fiery fineprint,

The Maker Makes No Guarantees,
though He promised

no more alluvial fits. In perpetual protest,
I shake my fist in air's congress and can't
help notice my hand made in His image
of finest clay and glaze—
it can reach and grip and hold its own,

rail at its Creator, O my palp and palm,
fortune's shape, stop, petition, clutch and escape.
And what of this prodigious foot? I stand
where I please, tread on this ledge
sketched in rime, perched halfway between

hope and failure.
And if able to pull myself up, I will—I will—

when it's time.

notes

p. 22: "Four": Number refers to preponderance of fours in Passover Seder: four questions, four sons/children.

p. 31: "Red Level": a draftsman's level.

p. 41: "Driving Lessons": a "big-macher" is Yiddish for an important, often public person or figure who generally lets you know that he or she is important.

p. 59: "Ketubah": the Jewish marriage contract.

p. 61: "Both to men and to women . . ." from 2 Samuel 6:19.

p. 63: "Where there is rejoicing, there should be trembling."Paraphrase from The Talmud, Berakhoth 30b: "When the son of Ravina was married, the father took a costly vase of white crystal, worth four hundred zuzim, and broke it before the rabbis present, who were in an uproarious mood, in order to curb their spirits." The custom has many interpretations, including: to fend off evil spirits (adopted from a German custom) and to remind of the destruction of the first and second temples.

p. 64: "Change of clothes? The very clothes of change." From James Merrill's poem, "Dreams About Clothes."

p. 66: "On the Wings of Every Kiss . . .": from "In a Sentimental Mood" by Duke Ellington, Emanuel Kurtz and Irving Mills, written in 1935.

p. 68: "And all the women went out after her with timbrels and with dances" from Exodus 15:20.

p. 69: "Rise up my love, my fair one, and come away": from Song of Songs 2:11.

p. 75: "A Golem's Lackey": The word golem shows up as an "unformed substance" in Psalm 139:16. In medieval Jewish legends, it represents an "artificial man" created by Kabbalistic (Jewish mystical) methods. Due to the heretical nature of suggesting that man can assume God's powers of creation, matters surrounding the Golem invariably run amuck. He is sometimes considered one of the models for Mary Shelley's *Frankenstein*.

p. 78: "Eighth Day": " . . . Between me and thee and thy seed after thee," is from Genesis 17:7.

p. 92: "Choir Rehearsal, 7 p.m.": The first stanza and continuing "exhortations" are patterned after Elizabeth Bishop's poem, "Invitation to Miss Marianne Moore"and borrows part of a line from that poem: ""The waves are running in verses . . ."

p. 94: "Learyic": an elegy for Timothy Leary.

p. 96: "Curriculum Vitae": In the Jewish mystical tradition, Adam Kadmon was the original, primordial man or "cosmic" man. Kabbalah also contains an extensive numerological tradition.

p. 99: "Manifesto of Regret and Acceptance": Tinkerbell is the tiny fairy in "Peter Pan" who dies if the children in the audience do not clap for her and proclaim, "I believe! I believe!"